Jeremy Lin

Jeremy Lin

Jeff Savage

MORGAN
REYNOLDS
PUBLISHING

Greensboro, North Carolina

Xtreme Athletes: Jeremy Lin

Copyright © 2013 by Morgan Reynolds Publishing

Library of Congress Cataloging-in-Publication Data

Savage, Jeff.
Jeremy Lin / by Jeff Savage.
  p. cm. -- (Xtreme athletes)
Includes bibliographical references and index.
ISBN 978-1-59935-352-4 -- ISBN 978-1-59935-353-1 (e-book) 1.
Lin,
Jeremy, 1988---Juvenile literature. 2. Basketball players--United
States--Biography--Juvenile literature. I. Title.
GV884.L586S38 2013
796.323092--dc23
[B]
                                      2012029417

Printed in the United States of America
First Edition

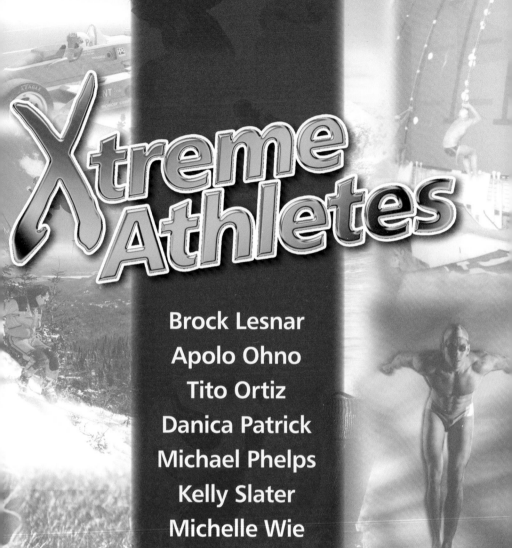

Xtreme Athletes

Brock Lesnar
Apolo Ohno
Tito Ortiz
Danica Patrick
Michael Phelps
Kelly Slater
Michelle Wie
Shaun White
Jeremy Lin

Contents

Jeremy Lin drives to the basket during the NBA All Star BBVA Rising Stars Challenge basketball game in Orlando, Florida, on February 24, 2012.

Palo Alto High School's Jeremy Lin celebrates victory at the California Interscholastic Federation state championship game on March 17, 2006.

one
Learning
the Game

Jeremy Lin pounded the basketball like a heavy metal drummer. At once, he dribbled past Derek Fisher and whirled around Kobe Bryant for the driving layup. The crowd at Madison Square Garden in New York roared in delight. Two weeks earlier, Jeremy was an unknown bench warmer for the New York Knicks. Now, as he led his team to a 2012 victory over the Los Angeles Lakers, he was igniting a firestorm of madness that would sweep the sports world. Amid booming chants of "M-V-P!" from delirious fans, Jeremy scored again and again, finishing off the Lakers and capturing the hearts of millions more who suddenly found themselves

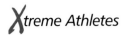

gripped by "Linsanity!" Jeremy's instant rise to global phenomenon was years in the making, and it began in Taiwan an era earlier.

Jeremy Shu-How Lin was born August 23, 1988, in Los Angeles, California. His father, Gie-Ming, and his mother, Shirley, emigrated from Taiwan to the United States in 1977. Both were computer engineers. Gie-Ming says he came to America for two reasons: to get his doctorate degree in engineering and "to watch the NBA." Gie-Ming enrolled at Purdue University in Indiana. After completing his PhD, he received his first job in Southern California, where Jeremy was born. Soon after, the Lin family moved to Northern California, where they made their home in Palo Alto. Jeremy has an older brother, Joshua, and a younger brother, Joseph.

Jeremy is the first American-born player of Taiwanese or Chinese descent. Taiwan and China are different countries, of course, so why are both mentioned? Lin's family history will explain. Gie-Ming's distant ancestors emigrated from Zhangpu County, Fujian, in mainland China in 1707. They were part of a mass wave of immigrants of that period, and most of today's Taiwanese residents

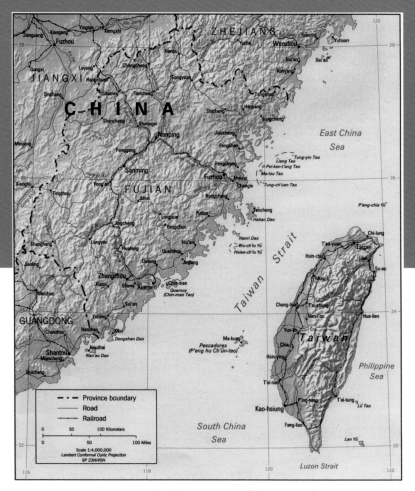

Taiwan is an island located just off the coast of China.

trace their ancestry to this migration from China. Meanwhile, Shirley's mother immigrated to Taiwan from Pinghu, Zhejiang, in mainland China in the late 1940s, at the end of China's civil war. Since both of Jeremy's parents grew up in Taiwan, and their ancestors came from China, it's no surprise that both countries proudly claim a stake in Jeremy's heritage.

Since both of Jeremy's parents worked, his grandmother, Lin Chu A Muen, came to California to help raise him and his brothers. She diapered and fed him, often cooking such Taiwanese dishes as fried rice with dried turnips and egg. She was over-protective, and she objected to Jeremy playing basketball as a young boy, out of concern that he would get hurt. But she was overruled by Jeremy's father, who insisted that his sons learn to play the game. Gie-Ming had seen glimpses of the NBA on television while in Taiwan, and when he moved to Los Angeles, he decided he wanted to start playing for fun. He had never touched a basketball in his life. He videotaped games and replayed the shooting styles of players in slow motion, and then he tried to copy their moves at a local gym. Like his wife, Gie-Ming was just five feet six inches tall, and he practiced for several years before he felt comfortable even playing in a pickup game.

When Joshua was five, his father began taking him to the local Y. Jeremy was next, and Joseph followed. "I realized that if I brought them from a young age, it would be like second nature for them," Jeremy's father said. "If they had the fundamentals, the rest would be easy." Jeremy was enrolled in a youth league at age five, and at first, Jeremy hardly knew why he was there. "He stood at half-court sucking his thumb for the entirety of about half his games that season," said Jeremy's brother, Josh. "It came to the point where my mom stopped going to watch his games." Midway through the season, Jeremy begged his mother to return to the Y to watch him play. Shirley told Jeremy that she would only go if he were going to try hard. "I'm going to play, and I'm going to score," he replied, according to Josh. In the next game, Jeremy scored the maximum number of points one player is permitted to score in the youth league. "From that game on," Josh said, "he just took off and never looked back."

Three nights each week after dinner, Jeremy went with his father and brothers to the Y to practice his dribbling and shooting. On Friday nights, after attending youth group meetings at the Chinese Church in Christ Mountain View, he would go with his brothers to a gym at Stanford University near his house, where they would play until two o' clock in the morning. On weekends, he sometimes spent all day playing in pickup games. "Ever since I was a little kid, I just loved to play this game," Jeremy said. "That's what I did for fun, all the time."

Before Jeremy reached middle school, Michael Jordan was leading the Chicago Bulls to a string of NBA titles. Jeremy dreamed of being like Mike. Jeremy's father put up a backboard and hoop in the family's backyard. Jeremy would play games with his brothers and friends while the Bulls game was on television. "We'd run to the window looking at what Jordan was doing, and we'd go out and do the move," Jeremy said. "And by the time we came back (to the window), they were on offense again, and so we'd end up watching basketball that way, and it was always a dream of mine."

Jeremy's dream seemed out of reach because he was so short. Jeremy's future high school coach, Peter Diepenbrock, remembers the first time he

Palo Alto High School head basketball coach Peter Diepenbrock

saw Jeremy play. "My first memory is of him coming to summer camp. He was a fifth grader," said Diepenbrock. "I just remember a really small player with a really nice feel for the game. He always had just a lot of confidence." When Jeremy tried out for the Palo Alto High team as a freshman, he stood five feet three. "Honestly, I didn't know if I was going to be able to play in high school," Jeremy said. "I was always one of the smallest guys. Every day I came home from practice asking my parents if I would grow taller." Jeremy made the team mainly because he was so skilled at the fundamentals of the game. He was a decent shooter, but his dribbling and passing skills were superior to other kids his age. In fact, he was so good that he got called up to the varsity squad for the playoffs. In the Vikings' first playoff game, he nailed a three-pointer down the stretch to help them win the game. At the team's postseason banquet, his coach announced, "Jeremy has a better skill set than anyone I've ever seen at his age."

Jeremy focused on academics, as was expected of him and his brothers, and he would eventually earn an outstanding 4.2 grade-point average in high school. But he was consumed now by basketball.

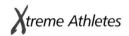

He had tacked posters of his favorite team—the local Golden State Warriors—on his bedroom wall, and he often stared from his bed at the players in the posters, imagining himself as them. If only he could grow taller. As a sophomore, he still stood five feet three inches. "I'm going to drink milk, and I'm going to become really tall!" he announced to his friend, Roger Chang. Maybe milk was Jeremy's secret potion. For whatever reason, he began to sprout rapidly. Within two years he grew an entire foot to his current height of six feet three. He maintained his agility as he grew, and his height allowed him more ways to maneuver through defenses, such as passing over an opponent rather than around him. As a junior, he was his varsity team's star point guard. Jeremy was having the time of his life, except for one thing: the insults. Asian Americans enjoy basketball as much as anyone, but at the time, they were a rare sight on hardwood courts. Jeremy heard the taunts from ignorant people in the stands. "Go back to China" and "Open your eyes," among others. Understandably, the insults stung. "It was definitely a lot tougher for me growing up," Jeremy said. "There was just an overall lack of respect." Being mocked for being different from others can be horribly painful, especially in high school. Jeremy's father gave his son excellent advice. "I told him people are going to say things to him, but he had to stay calm and not get excited by these words; they are only words," Gie-Ming said. "I told him to just win the game for your school and people will respect you." Jeremy tried to block out the taunts as best as he could. He was confident with his game, but out of self-protection, he carried it too far in his mind. He let his superior skills get the best of him to the point that he felt a superior attitude. It was a lapse of character and something his parents did not approve of. "I was just really arrogant," he admitted. Palo Alto had a chance to win the Northern California championship, but the night before the final game, Jeremy suffered a broken ankle. He was devastated. The injury proved to be an emotional turning point in his life. He discovered that he was not invincible. "It caused me to realize, this thing could be over at any minute," Jeremy said. "If I don't change my attitude, I'm going to look back and have a lot of regrets. That's when my whole attitude, not just to basketball but to life, changed." In the final against North Ridge High School, Jeremy sat on the bench dressed in

Mater Dei High's Travis Wear and Blake Arnet guard Palo Alto High's Jeremy Lin during the first half of the California Interscholastic Federation state championship game on March 17, 2006.

street clothes and tried to support his teammates any way he could. "He was so happy, and he was cheering as hard as he absolutely can," said teammate Brian Baskaukas. "In one way, I think that injury was sort of a turning point as far as maturation." The Vikings lost the game. But Jeremy's ankle healed, and he started his senior season with an equally determined, but quieter, confidence.

Palo Alto's 2005-06 basketball season was a parade. The Vikings went 32-1 as they sailed to the California state title. Jeremy orchestrated the offense with precision and flair, making split-second decisions that confounded defenses. Several times in the closing seconds, he rescued his team with some sort of heroic play. Trailing by two points to St. Francis High in the final minute of overtime, he nailed a twenty-five-foot three-pointer to win it. Behind by three points to Bakersfield High with five seconds left, he dribbled down the lane to draw two defenders and flicked a pass to suddenly wide-open teammate Steve Brown for a three-pointer at the buzzer to tie. Palo Alto won, 80-74, in overtime.

In the Northern California Division II semifinal game against Laguna Creek, the Vikings clung

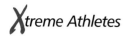

to a two-point lead in the final seconds. Brandon Adams was poised under the basket to go up for the tying basket when Jeremy swooped in and stole the ball. He was fouled, and his free throw iced the victory, 54-51. In the NorCal final against Mitty, the Vikings trailed by one point with twenty-four seconds left when Jeremy weaved his magic once again. He drove toward the basket to draw defenders toward him and whipped a pass to Brad Lehman for an open three-pointer and a 45-43 triumph.

All that remained was the California Inter-scholastic Federation Division II title game. Palo Alto's opponent was Mater Dei High, a nationally ranked powerhouse, and eight-time state champion. Mater Dei had seven players on its team who stood six feet seven or taller. Palo Alto was a heavy underdog. Even Jeremy knew it. He was surprised his team had even made it this far. "We would talk about winning the title," he said. "Deep down inside though, you're not fully expecting the victory because only one team in the entire state can win it. So, to be able to be there at that point in that tournament, to have that opportunity, I was, more than anything, just grateful. There were so many things that had to happen just perfectly. Tiny differences could have taken us out of contention for a championship."

Late in the game, which was played at Arco Arena in Sacramento, Palo Alto found itself staying right with the Monarchs. With two minutes left, Jeremy drilled a twenty-five-foot three-point bank shot. The Vikings held a slim two-point lead with thirty seconds left when Jeremy had the ball in his hands again. He dribbled toward the basket where he was confronted by Mater Dei star Taylor King. Rather than kick a pass out to a teammate this time, Jeremy took the ball strong over King for the basket that iced the game. Palo Alto won the title, 51-47. At the buzzer, Vikings fans stormed the court in celebration. Jeremy waved a black towel over his head and hugged his teammates. He had scored seventeen points, just above his average of 15.1 as a senior, to conclude a miraculous season. He also averaged 7.1 assists for the year, along with 6.2 rebounds and 5 steals. He was named first team all-state and was an easy choice as the Division II Player of the Year.

You would think that college recruiters would be crawling over one another to offer Jeremy an

athletic scholarship. Especially
with his stellar grades, Jeremy
would be sifting through a stack
of offers to attend the college
of his choice. This was not the
case. Jeremy did not receive a
single Division I scholarship
offer. Stanford University is
directly across the street from
Palo Alto High. But coach
Trent Johnson wouldn't cross
the street to invite him to play
for the Cardinal. "We knew all
about him," said Johnson. "But
nobody in the Bay Area . . . it
wasn't like there was any pressure on me to recruit him. There
was zero pressure. None."

Across the Bay is the
University of California at
Berkeley. But Cal coach Ben
Braun ignored Jeremy, too. "But
hey, I passed on Steve Nash,
too," admitted Braun. "We just
didn't extend Jeremy a scholarship. I love the kid, but we

Hoover Tower on the campus
of Stanford University

just didn't . . . I don't feel too bad. At least I'm not
the only one." Jeremy would have loved to play
at UCLA, where his brother, Josh, was attending. Kerry Keating, a Bruins assistant coach at the
time, even attended a game to watch Jeremy play.
Afterward, he told Jeremy, "We can't give you a
scholarship right away." Jeremy had done everything he could to get noticed. He even sent film of
himself to teams in the Ivy and the Patriot Leagues.
"He was a good student, a good player, and yeah,
it was amazing what he was doing," said Cornell
coach Steve Donahue. "But he didn't look that athletic and he didn't shoot it all that well."

Jeremy was discouraged by the utter lack
of interest. He felt invisible. He wasn't the tall-
est player, and he couldn't jump out of the gym,
so he knew he didn't have that "wow" factor that
can make a recruiter drool. "I just think in order
for someone to understand my game," Jeremy
explained, "they have to watch me more than
once, because I'm not going to do anything that's
extra flashy or freakishly athletic." There was
another reason why colleges probably gave Jeremy
the cold shoulder. It is not something recruiters
would admit, and perhaps some of them were not

even consciously aware that they were doing it. But Jeremy's experience was most likely a case of racial profiling. Being of Taiwanese decent placed him in a category that did not include basketball. "It's the Asian thing," said Rex Walters, a former NBA player who is Japanese American. "People who don't think stereotypes exist are crazy. If he's white, he's either a good shooter or heady. If he's Asian, he's good at math."

Rex Walters

Harvard assistant coach Bill Holden saw Jeremy play in an Amateur Athletic Union (AAU) tournament game. "He didn't really stand out," Holden said. "He was like any other average high school players we might see." Holden told Diepenbrock, Jeremy's high school coach, that Jeremy was only good enough to play at the Division III level. The next day, Holden saw Jeremy play in another game, this time against blue chip recruits. Another Harvard assistant, Lamar Reddicks, was also in attendance. This time, they saw Jeremy play with a killer instinct. "He was able to show his skill set," said Holden. "His ability to get to the rim, his ability to get into the lane and make some shots, and the ability to play some defense, which I didn't see him do the day before. His basketball knowledge and instincts for the game is what drew me to him." Jeremy immediately became Harvard's top recruit. As an Ivy League school, Harvard did not offer athletic scholarships. But by attending, Jeremy assured himself a top-flight education. "I just really wanted to go to Stanford," Jeremy said. "It was right across the street from my high school. I idolized Stanford players growing up. I didn't want to go to Harvard. That was, like, my last option." It turned out to be Jeremy's *only* option. In the summer of 2006, Jeremy packed his belongings and headed east. Next stop: Cambridge, Massachusetts.

Lin, playing for Harvard, dives for the ball during the second half of an NCAA basketball game in Boston.

two
Harvard
Education

Harvard University is the oldest institution of higher learning in the United States. It was founded in 1636. Lin embraced the school's rich history from the start. He especially appreciated the architecture on Harvard Yard along the Charles River.

Lin knew of Harvard's basketball history, as well. It certainly wasn't a hotbed for NBA players. The only players from the college to make it to the top pro league were Saul Mariaschin, who played for the Boston Celtics in 1947-48, Ed Smith, who played eleven games for the New York Knicks in 1953-54, and Wyndol Gray, who played for three teams over two years, starting with the Celtics. Knowing this, the NBA, though still a

dream for Lin, seemed farther away than ever. He held no illusions. For now, he was thankful to be issued uniform number four, the same jersey number he wore in high school. He did not expect to seize control of the team from the start. Nor did the Crimson coaches expect much from him. After all, he had a slight frame and a flawed jump shot. Assistant coach Reddicks said he was "the weakest guy on the team." But Lin did manage to get a decent amount of playing time. College games consist of two twenty-minute halves, and Lin averaged 18.1 minutes, or nearly half a game. He was the first guard off the bench, and he averaged 4.8 points, 2.5 rebounds, and 1.8 assists per game. His best statistic was his free throw percentage of 81.8. The Crimson finished with a 12-16 record, it's fifth losing season in a row, and afterward, head coach Frank Sullivan was fired.

As a sophomore, Lin was named the team's starting point guard by new coach Tommy Amaker. In the season's eighth game, he led the Crimson to a victory over Amaker's former team—the University of Michigan. Lin ended up starting all thirty games and averaged 12.6 points and 4.8 assists per game. Though the team struggled to an 8-22 record, it had suffered several close losses and had a nucleus of

Lin keeps the ball away from Michigan's Manny Harris in the second half of a basketball game in Boston.

young talent returning the next year. Lin was beginning to flourish, and he was named All-Ivy League
Second Team. Life seemed to be in his favor, with
one exception—the taunting. It was happening all
over again. Sure, it was a rare sight to see an Asian
American playing basketball at this level. As of
2010, less than 0.5% of men's Division I basketball
players were Asian American. But why did some
fans think that an anomaly was a license to ridicule? Lin said that he had to endure ethnic slurs
at nearly all Ivy League arenas. Shouts from the
stands like "Wonton soup" or "Sweet and sour pork"
or "Go back to China" were frequent. "It's everything you can imagine," Lin said. "Racial slurs,
racial jokes, all having to do with being Asian."
The insults would start as soon as Lin stepped onto
the court for warm-ups. Sometimes it wouldn't stop
until he left the floor at game's end. "They're yelling at me before, during, and after," he said. "I'm
an easy target because I'm Asian." It wasn't limited to East Coast colleges. During the summer, Lin
went home to the Bay Area, and while there, he
drove to Kezar Pavilion in San Francisco to play
in a Pro-Am game. "Sorry, sir," the guard at the
entrance told him as he approached, "there's no volleyball here tonight. It's basketball." Lin's religious

influence helped him cope with it. "We are called to turn the other cheek and love our enemies," he said. "It's just something I'm used to now, and it's a good opportunity to reflect the grace of God when you don't say anything back, or when you're really respectful in return. That says something powerful."

By now, Lin was a leader in Harvard's Asian American Christian Fellowship. He led campus prayer groups and Bible study sessions. He considered eventually becoming a pastor. In the meantime, he noticed that his approach to basketball was becoming more influenced in a religious way. "I learned more about a godly work ethic and a godly attitude, in terms of being humble, putting others above yourself, being respectful to refs and opponents," he said. "There are really so many ways you can apply your faith to basketball."

Lin had moved from the freshman dormitory to a residence at the edge of campus called Leverett House. Across the Charles River was Boston. Lin lived with a group of intelligent young men who were focused on academics but found time to socialize or play sports. Cheng Ho was a running back on the football team, and he and Jeremy became fast friends. Cheng taught Jeremy cool dance moves, and Jeremy influenced Cheng

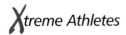

in a religious way. "The way he thinks and believes is very consistent," Cheng said, "and it's very contagious to be around him. I think what he has is a gift." Doug Miller, who shared team captain honors with Jeremy when they were seniors, also lived with him in Leverett House. Jeremy was eager to discuss religion, Miller said, but he never pushed his beliefs on others, and so he only talked about religion if another person brought up the subject. "He was just as willing to talk about Halo if that's what the other person wanted," Miller said. "We would also talk about girls or girl problems, video games, classes, or politics. He's a pretty smart guy."

Leverett House on Harvard's campus

Coach Amaker had been an outstanding play-making guard at Duke University, which is known for its powerhouse basketball program. Amaker took a special interest in helping develop Lin's skills. "Jeremy was a very, very driven kid," said assistant coach Will Wade. "He was a tremendous worker. He was always wanting to learn, always asking questions. Sometimes he would get frustrated with himself because he wasn't progressing at the rate he wanted to progress. For him, it was great having coach Amaker mentor him and guide him." With Amaker at Lin's side, it was no surprise that Lin's game blossomed by his junior season. He had always tried to dribble to the basket, but now he was slashing down the lane with an extra burst. His hard drives created more space for his teammates whose defenders would be forced to try to stop Lin's penetrating drives. Lin could take the ball to the rim and draw fouls. He could pass the ball to his teammates for open jumpers. He worked hard at the other end of the court and developed into a lockdown defender.

His skills were on full display in an early-January 2009 crosstown contest at Chestnut Hill against Boston College (BC). Three days earlier, the nationally ranked Eagles had defeated number

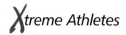

one-ranked North Carolina for their tenth straight win. Boston College was the heavy favorite, but Lin was not intimidated. From the start, he controlled the tempo of the game, determinedly dribbling the ball up the court. He set up at the top of the key and then slashed down the lane for layups or kick-out passes to an open teammate. Harvard built a 33-27 halftime lead. Lin's three-pointer from the left corner gave his team its first double-digit lead of the game, 42-31, with 16:55 to play. Boston College coach Al Skinner continually switched defenders on Lin. Nothing worked. "I tried to pre-warn them," Skinner said about the danger of taking Lin lightly. "He got in a rhythm." Lin racked up twenty-seven points, eight assists, six steals, and two blocked shots. On defense, he held BC All-America guard Tyrese Rice scoreless in the first half. Rice had scored twenty-five against top-ranked North Carolina. With four minutes left in the game, Rice still had just three points. Harvard won the game, 82-70. It was the school's first victory over a nationally ranked opponent in history.

The Crimson finished the season with a decent 14-14 record. Lin's individual statistics revealed his value to the team. He averaged 17.8 points, 5.5 rebounds, 4.3 assists, 2.4 steals, 0.6 blocked shots,

Lin drives for the basket in front of Boston College's Rakim Sanders in the first half of an NCAA college basketball game in Boston.

50.2 field goal percentage, 74.4 free throw percentage, and 40.0 three-point shot percentage. He
ranked in the top ten of his conference in every
one of these categories. He was the only Division I
player to do so.

As Lin's senior year arrived, he was on course
to graduate with a degree in economics. He had
also studied a breadth of curriculum, including the
Mandarin and Cantonese dialects of Chinese lin-
guistics. He was receiving an outstanding education,
just as his family had hoped for when he headed
east. While Lin knew he could land a fine job with
a Harvard degree, he wanted something different: a chance to play in the NBA. What seemed
almost preposterous three years ago—a player from
Harvard becoming a pro—seemed at least plausible
now.

Lin and his Crimson teammates won seven of
their first eight games to start the 2009-10 season.
Included in the streak was an 87-85 victory over
William & Mary in triple overtime. "He's a special
player who seems to have a special passion for the
game," said William & Mary coach Tony Shaver. "I
wouldn't be surprised to see him in the NBA one
day." Lin could do everything. He was second in
the Ivy League in scoring and steals, third in assists,
fifth in shooting percentage, sixth in blocked shots,

and tenth in rebounding. "He's as consistent as anyone in the game," said Amaker. "People who haven't seen him are wowed by what they see, but we aren't. What you see is who he is."

Lin played perhaps his best game next. The Crimson brought their 7-1 record to Storrs, Connecticut, to face the twelfth-ranked Huskies. UConn was led by superstar guard Kemba Walker and a mammoth front line. Lin didn't mind. With Walker trying to guard him, he kept his teammates involved by dishing out several assists, then scored seven straight points himself with a jump hook, a layup, and a three-pointer. Harvard trailed at half-time, 41-34. In the second half, Lin blocked shots, swallowed up rebounds, and went end-to-end with a dramatic dunk. With less than two minutes left, Harvard trailed, 71-62. Lin drilled a twelve-foot jumper. After a UConn free throw, Lin drained a twenty-five-foot, three-pointer to cut the lead to 72-67. UConn hit a pair of free throws, but Lin matched them with two free throws of his own. UConn hit two more free throws, but Lin answered with a dunk. UConn added more free throws, but Lin responded with another jump shot. Time finally ran out, with Harvard coming up short, 79-73. Afterward, all the talk was about Jeremy Lin. He had seized control of the game, scoring his team's

last eleven points, and finishing with a game-high thirty.
"I've seen a lot of teams come
through here, and he could
play for any of them," said
Hall of Fame Connecticut
coach Jim Calhoun. "He's got
great, great composure on the
court. He knows how to play."

Connecticut coach Jim Calhoun

Three days later, Lin and his teammates returned
to Chestnut Hill to the scene of their huge upset of
Boston College a year earlier. To show it wasn't a
fluke, they stunned the Eagles again. Lin scored
a game-high twenty-five points as Harvard controlled the second half in a 74-67 victory. Lin played
his best in his team's biggest games, and even he
couldn't help but wonder why. "There are times
when I'm out there on the basketball court, and it
feels like I'm not even controlling my own body," he
said. "It's almost as though someone else is using
me as a puppet. There are things I do that, when I
look at them afterwards, I wonder how I did that. In
moments like that, I realize that there is something
more to what's happening around me, something
supernatural about it."

Lin averaged 16.4 points and 4.5 assists in leading Harvard to a superb 21-8 season. The Crimson
lost key games down the stretch to Cornell and

Princeton to finish 10-4 in the Ivy League. They were
invited to play in the postseason College Basketball
Invitational, and their season ended with a first-round
loss to Appalachian State. Lin's personal ascension to
the top of the Ivy League was clear: he had become
the first player in league history to record at least 1,450
points, 450 rebounds, and 400 assists. He was one of
eleven finalists for the coveted Bob Cousy Award as
the nation's most valuable player. His accomplishments

The Bob Cousy Award is an annual basketball award given to the top
men's collegiate point guard. It is named after six-time NBA champion Bob
Cousy, (left), who played point for the Boston Celtics from 1951 to 1963
and won six championships.

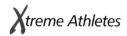

had turned conventional thinking by basketball purists on its ear. "It's a sport for white and black people," Lin simply said. "You don't get respect for being an Asian American basketball player in the U.S." With Lin's records now on display for all to see, he thought he was headed to the NBA.

Lin had prepared himself for just such an arrangement. He had secured an agent to handle his business matters. Roger Montgomery contacted Lin after watching him dissect the UConn defense a few months earlier. "Right away, I liked his game," said Montgomery. "I thought, 'I've got to get him.' Often, I don't bother going after top prospects. I aim for guys who are similar to me: they haven't been given much in their careers and they're super motivated to prove themselves." Lin signed with Montgomery in April 2010. The NBA draft was approaching, and both men knew they faced another hurdle. The Ivy League had long been per-ceived as an inferior conference with less athletic players. "There are very few guys from the Ivy League that have made it, and it's because of the power conferences," Orlando Magic assistant gen-eral manager Dave Twardzik said. "The Ivy League players are at a disadvantage in terms of television exposure." Indeed, the NBA had not drafted an Ivy

League player since Jerome Allen of Penn in the second round in 1995. The last Ivy League player to play in the NBA was Yale's Chris Dudley in 2003. The last Harvard player was Ed Smith in 1954. That is a glaring disadvantage.

The NBA draft would be held June 24, 2010. In the meantime, Lin was invited to play in the Portsmouth Invitational, a predraft camp that featured sixty-four college players who were essentially put on display to showcase their skills for NBA coaches and scouts. The invited players were not the top draft picks. They were fringe players, with an average of one in ten getting drafted. For instance, six of the sixty-four players from the previous year's camp were drafted, all six in the second round. Lin played point guard and shooting guard well enough to be noticed by several teams. In three games, he averaged 10.3 points and 6.0 assists. Right before the draft, each team holds special workouts at their home arena to evaluate potential picks. Eight pro teams invited Lin to their workouts. The problem for Lin was that these workouts were not full-court games of five-on-five, but rather, one-on-one, two-on-two, or three-on-three half-court contests. They were structured to analyze athletic ability over some of Lin's main strengths,

New York Knicks coach
Mike D'Antoni

such as court awareness and vision. Still, Lin thought he made a decent impression, and he was especially heartened when New York Knicks coach Mike D'Antoni called him into his office after his workout and told him he saw "some Steve Nash-type qualities." The Knicks were looking to upgrade their point guard position, and Lin thought he was a perfect fit. The Knicks might even take him the first round, he thought.

The draft was held in the Theatre at Madison Square Garden in New York City. Many college players who were certain early choices were invited to attend. Lin was not among them. He sat at home on his couch and watched on television. He texted with Montgomery. The first round passed. There was one round to go. The Knicks held two second-round picks. They used their first one to select Landry Fields, a shooting guard from Stanford, and a friend of Lin's. More teams passed on Lin. Eight picks or

Landry Fields

so into the second round, Mavericks general manager Donnie Nelson called Lin to tell him that while the Mavs would not be selecting him, Nelson wanted to invite him to try out as a free agent. Nelson mentioned something about a summer league. "I guess he already knew I wasn't going to be drafted," Lin said. Sure enough, the Knicks used their second pick on guard Andy Rautins. Lin went undrafted. "I was devastated," Montgomery said. "There were sleepless nights." Lin remembered this feeling all too well. It was as though he was reliving his nightmare from high school, when he played magnificently, yet was ignored by colleges. How could no NBA team want him? "I was very disappointed. Discouraged," Lin said. "I'm undrafted. Out of Harvard. Asian American. That was kind of the perception that everyone had of me, and that was the perception that I had of myself, and when everyone thinks that, it's hard to break that."

Lin poses with his parents, Gie-ming, (*right*), and Shirley, (*left*), during a news conference at the Golden State Warriors' headquarters in Oakland, California, on July 21, 2010.

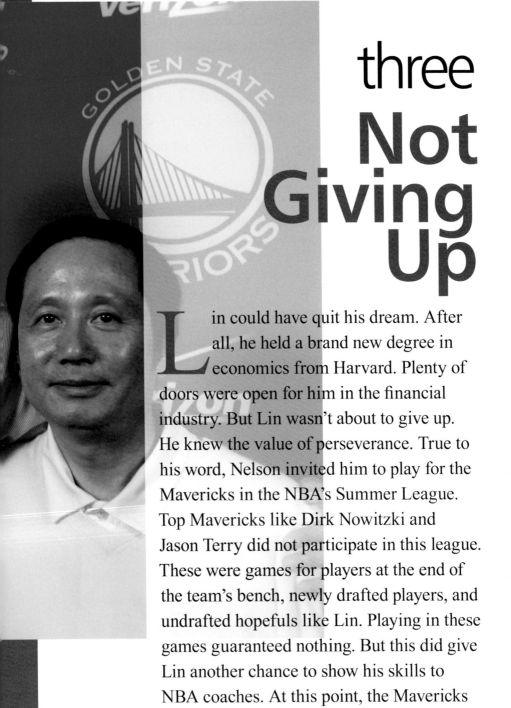

three
Not Giving Up

Lin could have quit his dream. After all, he held a brand new degree in economics from Harvard. Plenty of doors were open for him in the financial industry. But Lin wasn't about to give up. He knew the value of perseverance. True to his word, Nelson invited him to play for the Mavericks in the NBA's Summer League. Top Mavericks like Dirk Nowitzki and Jason Terry did not participate in this league. These were games for players at the end of the team's bench, newly drafted players, and undrafted hopefuls like Lin. Playing in these games guaranteed nothing. But this did give Lin another chance to show his skills to NBA coaches. At this point, the Mavericks

did not own the rights to Lin. He was free to sign with any team. The Mavs were simply the team that was providing him this opportunity. "Donnie took care of me. He really, really did," Lin said. "I'm not just saying that. And I'm thankful to him. He has a different type of vision than most people do. He saw potential in me."

Lin played in five summer league games in Las Vegas. He was used at both guard positions to gauge his versatility. Although he was on the court for just 18.6 minutes per game, in that brief window he averaged 9.8 points and 3.2 rebounds, 1.8 assists, and 1.2 steals. Most impressive, he led his team with a blistering 54.5 shooting percentage. His most eye-opening performance came against the Washington Wizards. He was matched against superstar John Wall from Kentucky, the number one pick in the draft. During introductions, Wall received the loudest cheer for any player. By the end of the game, the cheering was for Lin. He had outplayed Wall, holding him to just 4-for-19 shooting. He even out-jumped Wall, who reportedly had a forty-three-inch vertical jump, on a jump ball. On offense, Lin was 6-for-12 from the floor in twenty-eight minutes. He was especially effective in the fourth quarter when he torched the top pick with eleven points. "That was by far the biggest thing for

Washington Wizards' John Wall

me in terms of my stock and everything," Lin said.
"Just thank God for a perfect performance on a perfect night. The timing of that was unbelievable."
NBA teams certainly noticed Lin now. "He showed
us that he can be an NBA point guard," said one
team scout. "He showed us he can finish, defend,
and has above-average athleticism."

Roger Montgomery's phone started to ring. NBA teams were suddenly calling. The Mavericks offered to sign Lin to a contract. So did the Los Angeles Lakers and an unnamed team from the Eastern Conference. Then the Golden State Warriors called. Golden State, of course, was Lin's favorite team growing up in the Bay Area. Lin was offered a two-year contract for $500,000 to sign with the Warriors. At least half the money was guaranteed, meaning that if Lin got cut at any point, he could keep that portion. Lin says he was offered more money by other teams, but that he really wanted to play for his favorite team. He agreed to join the Warriors. A press conference was held at the team's complex in Oakland. Television crews and news reporters packed the building. "It was surprising to see that we had almost a full-blown media day, with a bunch of national media here, for an undrafted rookie," Warriors coach Keith Smart said. The attention on Lin was just beginning. Nike signed him to a three-year contract to sponsor their athletic equipment. His number seven Warriors jersey went on sale before he took his first dribble. Training camp opened with some fans blogging that Lin would be the point guard to rescue the Warriors from years of futility. Lin kept things in perspective.

Jeremy Lin at the 2010 Golden State Warriors' open practice.

"I've got news for them," he said, smiling. "I won't be an All-Star this year."

The Warriors were longtime losers, making the playoffs just once in the previous sixteen years. Even so, they did boast two promising young guards—Monta Ellis and Stephen Curry. Lin knew his opportunity to play would be limited; he was just hoping to stick with the team. At the team's first practice, coach Smart observed that Lin wasn't intimidated by the reputation of Ellis and Curry. Time after time he slashed into the lane for shots. "He's getting to the paint," Smart said. "You say, 'Man, that's a unique skill.' Now he needs to pass the ball, as opposed to trying to get to the rim all the time." Smart soon learned something else about his new rookie—a solid work ethic. Lin was the first player at the training facility every day, arriving at 8:30 a.m. "All of a sudden you'd hear a ball bouncing on the floor," the coach said. It was Lin's dribbling. Practice did not start until noon.

Golden State's season opened with a win against the Houston Rockets. Lin sat at the end of the bench and cheered for his team but did not play. Two nights later, on October 29, 2010, the Los Angeles Clippers arrived in town. The Warriors were hosting their annual Asian Heritage Night. Oracle Arena was filled with 17,408 fans. It was estimated that at least 2,000 had come to represent the large Asian community in the Bay Area. Midway through the fourth quarter, with the Warriors comfortably in the lead, the crowd started to chant, "We want Lin!" With two and a half minutes to go, Smart reached for Lin. The crowd stood and cheered as Lin walked to the scorer's table. At the next whistle, he stepped onto the court as his name was announced over the arena's public address system. The crowd roared. With that, it was official. Lin had become the first American-born player of Taiwanese or Chinese decent to play in an NBA game. At a question-and-answer session after the game in front of more than one thousand appreciative fans, he was asked how he felt at that precise moment. "I sat on the bench for awhile, so I went from completely dry to completely soaked with sweat in a split second after I heard the ovation," Lin said to laughter from the crowd. "I just had so much adrenaline going through me."

Lin handled the ball several times. He even called out a few plays while dribbling to settle the offense. He did not attempt a shot, but he did get credit for his first NBA steal when he controlled a jump ball. He got to dribble out the last few seconds of the game in a Warriors 109-91 victory. Afterward, he told reporters, "I'm thankful to my

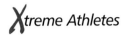

parents and everyone, my brothers, my friends, and my coaches—everyone that has helped me get to this point. I'm just very thankful, that's all I can really say. I'm just thankful for everything."

The Warriors traveled to Los Angeles to play their first road game against the Lakers. Coach Smart used Lin more this time, playing him for sixteen minutes, including eleven in the twelve-minute third quarter. Lin played with energy, dishing out three assists, and making four steals. He missed four of his five shots. Although the Warriors got blown out, 107-83, he showed he could compete by leading his team on a 12-1 run midway through the third quarter. On one play, he dived to the floor to wrestle the ball away from power forward Lamar Odom, and then, while seated, threw a pass to teammate Brendan Wright for a dunk. Less than thirty seconds later, he scored on a fast-break layup for his first NBA basket. Reporters swarmed him afterward, and he tried his best to deflect attention. "I'm not going to really talk about what I did personally when we lost by 24," he said. "I'm just learning slowly the NBA game."

Lin's performance impressed the Lakers. Veteran point guard Derek Fisher was eager to offer praise. "He plays with good energy. He's aggressive.

He's not afraid of the competition. Those are good things to have when you're a young player regardless of where you're from," said Fisher, who understood the magnitude of Lin's presence in the league. "He's carrying the hopes of an entire continent. He's accomplished a lot more than I have already. He just has to keep working hard and remain confident in himself. He's here for a reason."

Derek Fisher

Asian Americans in the NBA

On October 29, 2010, Jeremy Lin stepped onto the court for the Golden State Warriors to become just the fourth Asian American to play in the NBA.

The first was Wataru "Wat" Misaka, a Japanese American born in Utah. At five feet seven, Misaka led the University of Utah to the 1944 NCAA Tournament title. He served the next two years in the U.S. Army, rising to the rank of staff sergeant, then returned to Utah where he led the Utes to the 1947 NIT title. He was drafted by the New York Knicks but played in only three games, scoring seven points, before he was cut.

Raymond Townsend was born in San Jose, California, to an American father and a Filipina mother. He played on UCLA coach John Wooden's final NCAA championship team in 1975. The Golden State Warriors drafted the six-foot-three-inch-tall point guard with the twenty-second pick in the first round of the 1978 draft. Townsend played three seasons for the Warriors and one with the Indiana Pacers, with a career average of 4.8 points per game.

Rex Walters was born in Omaha, Nebraska, and his Caucasian father and Japanese mother raised him in San Jose. A six-foot-four guard, he played from 1993-2000 for the New Jersey Nets, Philadelphia 76ers, and Miami Heat, averaging 4.6 points per game. He is currently head coach at the University of San Francisco. "I am a Japanese American, I take great pride in that," Walters said. "We got a guy like Jeremy Lin breaking barriers, I'd like to think I played a small part in that."

Other Asians who were not born in America have played in the NBA, the most notable being seven-foot-six-inch center Yao Ming from China, who starred for the Houston Rockets before retiring in 2011. Jeremy says he talks with Yao by telephone after every game, calling him a mentor and a friend.

In the next nine games, Lin played a total of just thirty-four minutes, mostly in "garbage time" when the game's outcome had already been decided. He remained a fan favorite at home, and some in the media even dubbed Oracle Arena "Roaracle." Each time Lin entered a game, the crowd howled with delight. "I've never seen that kind of reception for a rookie," veteran teammate David Lee said. "Jeremy has a cult following."

Curiously, Lin performed better away from home. His teammates understood why. "There's a lot of pressure on him at home, with all of the applause for just checking into the game, so I'm sure that cranks up his nerves a little bit," said guard Stephen Curry. "You can tell on the road he plays a lot better, because he can just go out there, play, and have fun." When Lin was asked by reporters to address the issue, he knew he wanted to be careful with what he said. He truly appreciated the support of the fans. He certainly

Stephen Curry during a game between the Golden State Warriors and the Washington Wizards

didn't want to appear ungrateful. "When I'm on the road, I don't feel like the spotlight is on me," is how he put it. By now, Lin's story had become such a hot topic that he was bombarded with interview requests in every city the Warriors visited. Golden State's media relations staff had to decline most requests to allow Lin time to work on his game.

Lin spent endless hours studying film of the league's top point guards. He worked closely with assistant coaches Stephen Silas and Lloyd Pierce, practicing the timing of the pick-and-roll, a play that involves two players. He perfected keeping the defender on his hip while drawing the bigger inside defender toward him and then dishing the pass at just the right instant to his pick-and-roll teammate. He also spent a lot of time on his long-range shooting, because in the words of coach Smart, "Jeremy couldn't shoot at all." His progress was slow and steady. Eventually, the coaches figured Jeremy would benefit more from playing full time in the Development League than picking up a few minutes of garbage time with the Warriors. Each NBA team has a lower-level team, similar to Major League Baseball's minor leagues. Jeremy was sent to Golden State's D-League affiliate in Reno, Nevada. While playing for the Reno Bighorns, he worked with coach Eric Musselman on aspects of his offense like using the entire half court rather than just one side of it. Musselman was encouraged by one aspect of Lin's game, saying, "I thought he was one of the best dribble-drive guys I ever coached."

Lin returned to the Warriors and enjoyed moderate success in limited playing time, and his best performance came at the Staples Center again against the Lakers, where he scored a season-high thirteen points by making four of nine shots and all five of his free throws. He was sent to Reno again for more game action, and during this stint he and Musselman expanded on the pick-and-roll by working on a move mastered by superstar point guard Chris Paul in which the play is started just beyond half court. It didn't take Lin long to grasp the move. "That was the point when we knew that he was a special player," said Musselman. "Because the more wide open the floor

Chris Paul (center)

was, the better he became." Lin also worked on getting off the shot after absorbing contact from big interior defenders on drives to the basket. He also learned how to read traps and forms of double-teams better. The practice was invaluable.

NBA players are afforded such luxuries as flying on chartered planes with spacious seating. D-League teams

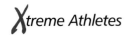

take commercial flights. One perk for any D-League player who has played even one game in the NBA is to get first-class tickets. Lin always gave his first-class ticket to a teammate. He did not want special treatment. He preferred squeezing into a standard coach seat. He was recalled by the Warriors, but after a few games spent mostly seated toward the end of the bench, was back with the Bighorns once more, this time primarily to straighten out his body on his jump shot. His knees bent too much, and his arm angle was too far behind his head. Lin trusted his coaches by totally reworking the style he had used all his life. In twenty games with Reno, he averaged 18 points, 5.8 rebounds, and 4.4 assists. He returned to Oakland to finish the season with the Warriors and played his most minutes—twenty-four, or exactly half of a game—in the season finale against the Portland Trail Blazers at Oracle. He made five of eight shots for twelve points and had five rebounds and five assists.

From training camp to the playoffs, the NBA season stretches nine months. Most players take the summer off. Such an idea never crossed Lin's mind. He sought to improve his game with the help of expert coaches near his Palo Alto home. Doc Scheppler was a long-shot guru, and Lin worked out in Scheppler's backyard in Burlingame. Lin learned to start his shooting motion earlier and release it at the peak of his jump. He played a game called "beat the ghost," in which he earned one point for every shot he made from beyond the three-point arc and lost three points to the "ghost" for every miss. Lin knew the odds were stacked against him. After all, he was an economics major. But he refused to quit until he beat the ghost. In one game, he drained seventeen three-pointers but lost, 21-17. He kicked the ball in frustration. He played fourteen games until he finally won. "That's the beauty of Jeremy Lin," Scheppler said. "It's not about moral victories. It's 'I have to win.'"

Lin also needed to improve his strength, especially while driving down the lane. He worked with Phil Wagner, a physician and trainer in Menlo Park, who implemented a training program for Lin involving heavy weights and low repetitions. Before long, Lin more than doubled the amount of weight he could squat, from 110 pounds to 230, and he increased the number of pull-ups he could do from twelve to thirty. By the end of the summer, he had added twelve pounds of muscle to his frame while increasing his standing vertical jump three and a half inches. "Before, he was a motorcycle—he was maneuverable, but very off-balance," said Wagner. "Now he's like a Porsche—he's fast, but he's stable. When he gets into traffic, he's able to maintain his direction and his balance because he's stronger."

Lin was eager to put his improvements to the test, but he began to wonder when he would get that chance.

The NBA's players and owners did not have a working agreement, and through their attorneys, they negotiated over issues like revenue sharing, a salary cap, and a luxury tax. In other words, they argued over money. The start of the 2011-12 NBA season was in the lurch. In late September, Lin traveled to Guangzhou, China, where he played in a few games for the Dongguan Leopards. Lin played point guard and led the Leopards to the Asian Basketball Association Championship title game, where they lost, 72-69. Even in defeat, Lin was an easy choice as the tournament's Most Valuable Player.

While in China, Lin was urged by Shanghai Sharks team president Yao Ming to sign a contract to play for the Sharks. Yao was the seven-foot-six certain Hall of Fame center for the Houston Rockets who had retired a year earlier. Yao knew that getting Lin would be a coup for the Chinese league. But Lin had his sights set on the NBA, if the owners and players could settle their differences, and so he declined Yao's offer.

Yao Ming

Lin returned to the United States and immediately resumed his intense workouts. The NBA season was scheduled to start November 1, but that date passed, and the players were "locked out." This meant that they were not allowed to use their teams' practice facilities or have any contact with the coaches or training staff. The season would be shortened, if it were played at all. The Warriors coaches had heard about Lin's improvements, but they had not actually seen him firsthand. After more haggling by attorneys, a new deal, called a collective bargaining agreement, was tentatively reached in late November. The season would be shortened from its usual eighty-two-game schedule to sixty-six. Team owners allowed players to hold voluntary workouts starting December 1. An agreement was officially signed one week later. On December 9, the NBA was officially back in business. Training camp opened. Teams started making trades.

The Warriors needed help at center. They had their eye on free agent center DeAndre Jordan. To prevent one team from signing too many superstars, a limit is placed on the amount of money it can spend on players. This is called the salary cap. The Warriors were near the top of their salary cap. In order for them to offer Jordan a rich contract, they needed to cut their payroll. The first move the Warriors made on December 9 was strictly a business decision: *They cut Jeremy Lin.*

Fans cheer for New York Knicks point guard Jeremy Lin during the second half of an NBA basketball game against the Washington Wizards in Washington.

four
Seizing the Opportunity

Technically, the Warriors placed Lin on the waiver wire. This meant that any other team could claim the rights to him, for his existing salary. If he were not claimed within forty-eight hours, he would become a free agent and could sign with any team that wanted him. Lin was due to earn $788,000, and the Warriors wanted to put that money toward their offer to Jordan. New Warriors owner Joe Lacob preferred keeping Lin, and he asked team officials to try to come up with other options. They couldn't. Lin was in the middle of practice when he was pulled aside and told that he was being let go. He was crushed. He cleaned out his locker and drove home. When a newspaper reporter asked him later about how he felt, Lin

could have sulked. Instead, he maintained a positive attitude. "It was a calculated business decision they made to benefit the team. I have no hard feelings," he said. "I'm so thankful for the Warriors fans, I have no way I can even express it."

Two days later, Lin was on an airplane to Houston. The Rockets had claimed him. That same day, the Warriors offered DeAndre Jordan a four-year deal worth $43 million. The next day, the Los Angeles Clippers matched the offer. Jordan signed with the Clippers. The Warriors gave up Lin for nothing.

Lin arrived in Houston where he checked into a hotel. He joined the Rockets for practice the next day. Houston already had three point guards on the team with guaranteed contracts. Kyle Lowry was an emerging star. Goran Dragic was a talented backup. Jonny Flynn had just been acquired in a trade. Lin wondered where he would fit in.

Lin as a Houston Rocket

The Rockets must have wondered, too. Lin played in two exhibition games for a total of seven minutes—and then *the Rockets cut him*. It was a salary cap issue again. The Rockets needed to clear space on their payroll to sign center Samuel Dalembert. Lin was officially placed on waivers on Christmas Day. A normally joyful time was reduced to dread. In bed that night, Lin cried. Questions raced through his mind. "If I don't have a team, what's going to happen?" he wondered. "Do I go to the D-League? Do I go overseas? Do I take a break altogether?" Doubt overwhelmed him.

The next day, Roger Montgomery got a phone call. Lin's agent noticed the area code. "When I saw the 212 on my phone, I thought, 'Here we go. Let's see what happens.'" The call was coming from New York City. The Knicks were on the phone. Coach Mike D'Antoni remembered certain qualities about Lin from the team's special workout a year earlier. "We did like his playmaking ability," D'Antoni said. "We liked his ability to get in the paint. We liked that he was unselfish. We liked that he was smart. We liked that he had all the intangibles of being a point guard." But D'Antoni and his staff also had questions about Lin's ability. "We didn't know if he could defend well enough," said the coach. "We didn't know whether he could finish well enough.

And we didn't know if he could shoot outside well enough."

The Knicks were willing to take a chance. They needed a healthy body. Iman Shumpert, their promising rookie point guard, had suffered a knee injury in a game the day before. Veteran Baron Davis had been signed one week earlier, but he wouldn't be ready to play for at least two months due to a back injury. Toney Douglas and Mike Bibby were decent backups who would fill in while Shumpert and Davis healed. Lin would serve as an emergency backup, in case something happened to either of them. In a whirlwind of events, Lin suddenly found himself back in the Bay Area, joining his third team in a month. He was assigned jersey number seventeen for the Knicks. His opponent? The Warriors—at Oracle Arena. "Everything I expected coming into this season has been flipped upside down," Lin said. The Knicks were promptly blown out, 92-78. With the game out of reach, Lin was inserted with 1:27 to play. He was greeted with cheers from the crowd, and he immediately put up a nineteen-foot jump shot that missed. He didn't shoot again. Afterward, reporters speculated that Lin wouldn't get to play much until he learned the Knicks playbook. "He's from Harvard," D'Antoni joked. "It will take him about an hour and a half."

Lin shoots over David Lee of the Golden State Warriors.

The coach did confess that Lin would play only under desperate circumstances. "If somebody wakes up with a cold, he's playing a lot," D'Antoni said. "If not, we'll see." Sure enough, Lin played just two minutes in a loss at the Lakers and four minutes in a win at the Sacramento Kings to conclude the team's road trip. Lin flew back to New York with his new teammates and headed to his brother Josh's apartment. Josh was a dental student at New York University, living in a one-bedroom apartment on Manhattan's Lower East Side. Josh's living room would serve as Lin's new home. His couch would be Lin's bed.

"I'm still kind of in shock," Lin admitted to the New York media. "I'm just going to play basketball. I'm not going to over think anything. I'm just going to go out there, have some fun, and play." Actually, Lin sat. For the next three games, he never left his seat at the end of the bench, except to greet his teammates during timeouts. At the end of a blowout win in Detroit, he entered the game with four minutes left and scored his first basket as a Knick on a driving layup. He added two free throws to finish with four points. He was confined to the bench again for three games before playing the final 4:41 at Oklahoma City. The Thunder were ahead by twenty-two points, but Lin would lead the reserves on a 15-5 run to close the game in a 104-92 loss. He scored on a layup, made a free throw, grabbed a defensive rebound, and threw a pass to Jerome Jordan for a dunk on the game's final play. Three days later, he was sent to the Erie BayHawks—the Knicks' D-League affiliate. Lin tried to look at his situation positively. With the BayHawks, at least he would get to play more. He seized the opportunity by recording a triple-double with twenty-eight points, eleven rebounds, and twelve assists in a 122-113 victory over the Maine Red Claws. The Knicks immediately recalled him. In a blowout win over the lowly Charlotte Bobcats, Lin was put in the game with 5:52 left. He immediately threw a pass to Steve Novak for a three-pointer. One minute later, he rose up and nailed a seventeen-foot jumper. He assisted Novak again for another three-pointer, then he drove to the rim himself, drew the foul, and hit both free throws. At the defensive end, he blocked Bismack Biyombo's six-footer. He nailed a nine-footer. He assisted Novak for a third three-pointer. He drew another foul and converted both free throws. He rebounded Charlotte's last miss to end the game. On a night when Knicks leading scorer Carmelo Anthony was held to a career-low one point, Lin scored eight points, and the Knicks won by thirty-three. But New York's next two games were tighter, and Lin was confined to the bench again.

Lin moved in with teammate Landry Fields. He slept in the living room of Fields's apartment, but at least Fields had a longer couch. Lin was earning enough money to rent his own apartment but for how long? A crucial date was approaching. Lin's contract was not guaranteed, meaning that if he were cut, the Knicks would not have to pay him the remainder of his salary. Teams had until February 7 to cut players with nonguaranteed contracts. After that date, they were obligated to pay a player's entire salary for that year, even if they got cut at a

later date. This was the business part of the NBA that most fans don't see.

In Miami on January 27, Lin went to a pregame chapel with teammates Landry Fields and Jerome Jordan, along with Heat forward Udonis Haslem. At the service, Lin asked the chaplain and his fellow worshippers to pray that the Knicks wouldn't cut him. He did not play that night against the Heat, but the following night in Houston, coach D'Antoni put Lin into the game with eight minutes left in the third quarter. Lin never left the court. He played twenty straight minutes. Why? Iman Shumpert had rejoined the team as the starting point guard. But the Knicks weren't getting much production from their backups. Mike Bibby had proven to be old and ineffective. Toney Douglas had regressed, as well. Against the Rockets, Lin scored nine points and had six assists. But he was only three-for-nine shooting and committed three turnovers. Such mixed results were not inspiring to the Knicks coaches. Lin was given just thirteen minutes of playing time over the next three games. It was the third game that tipped the scales in his favor once and for all.

At the TD Garden in Boston, Lin was put into the game against the Celtics with 2:38 left in the first quarter to replace Shumpert. It was the first time he had entered a game so early. He immediately committed a turnover and then fouled Paul Pierce. But he rectified those errors by drawing a foul right before the first-quarter buzzer and making both free throws. In the first minute of the second quarter, he grabbed a defensive rebound and assisted on a layup

Paul Pierce

by Amar'e Stoudemire. He pulled down one more rebound before being replaced four minutes into the second quarter. He did not return. The Knicks held the lead through three quarters, but sloppy play allowed the Celtics to come back and win the game, 91-89. The Knicks had lost eleven of their last thirteen games to see their record fall to 8-15.

There was media speculation that coach D'Antoni could get fired if he didn't find a way to turn things around. The team's point guard play was subpar. The deadline to cut players to save

money was in three days. Coach D'Antoni said it was for these reasons that he decided to give Lin one more long look the following night. If Lin thought his life had been flipped upside down before, it didn't compare to what would happen next. The entire sporting universe was about to be flipped upside down.

Madison Square Garden was filled with 19,763 fans. The New Jersey Nets were in town. The Nets were led by star point guard Deron Williams. With 3:34 left in the first quarter, the Knicks already were behind, 21-16. That's when Lin replaced Shumpert. By the end of the quarter, the Knicks trailed by ten. Then everything Lin had always known—his court awareness and slashing style— and all of his improvements (his extended pick-and-roll, his squats and vertical jump, his beating the ghost) it all came together in one glorious display. Call it supernatural. Call it the result of endless hours of resilience and hard work. Whatever it was, it manifested itself beneath the giant pinwheel ceiling of the world's most famous arena for all to see.

Lin played the entire second quarter and had a team-high six points and three assists, including a lob to Tyson Chandler for a tying dunk at forty-six with 1:32 left. At halftime, Carmelo Anthony suggested to D'Antoni that Lin should play more in the second half. Shumpert started the third quarter, but after a bad pass and a missed layup, Lin was back on the court. With 2:34 left, he drove hard past Williams for the basket and the foul. His three-point play cut New Jersey's lead to 66-62. With three seconds left in the quarter, he powered over Keith Bogans to the rim for another three-point play to get the Knicks to within two, 72-70.

The Knicks weren't getting much help from their two usual stars. Anthony would contribute just 3-of-15 shooting, and Stoudemire would play just thirteen minutes the first three quarters due to foul trouble. Lin didn't seem to mind who was on the court with him. After a Jared Jeffries tip shot to open the fourth quarter tied it, Lin calmly drilled a nineteen-footer to give the Knicks the lead. The public address announcer boomed "Jeremy Linnnnn!" The Garden seemed to be shaking. Midway through the quarter, he knocked down a fourteen-footer and then drove along the baseline and fed Stoudemire for a layup and an 84-82 lead. With Williams in his face, he scored on a soft floater to make it 86-82. Chants of "Jer-e-my!" filled the arena. With 3:25 left, his free throw made it 92-86. After a series of misses, he had the ball again. He powered down the lane past Williams and got fouled by Anthony Morrow, but he was

New Jersey Nets' Jordan Williams avoids fouling Lin during the second quarter of an NBA basketball game at Madison Square Garden in New York.

strong enough to put the ball up and in. The crowd roared as he converted the free throw for the three-point play and a 95-86 lead. The Nets called time out with the Garden crowd dancing.

On New York's next possession, he drove hard again for another basket. The Knicks won, 99-92. Lin's teammates hugged him at center court as Pearl Jam's song "Jeremy" blasted from the sound system. He had scored a career-high twenty-five points while holding Williams to 7-for-19 shooting. "A little overwhelmed right now," Lin said to the crush of reporters in the locker room. "I'm still kind of in shock by everything that happened." TV crews and other media blocked Stoudemire's path to his locker. "What's going on, Jeremy? Can I have my locker back?" he joked. Stoudemire called Jeremy's performance "phenomenal." Coach D'Antoni was thrilled to know that the answer to his point guard woes had been sitting at the end of the bench all along. "The biggest thing is, he's got a point-guard mentality," said the coach. "He has a rhyme or reason to what he's doing. It's something we sorely needed."

At practice the next day, D'Antoni told reporters that he was thinking of starting Lin in the following night's game at the Garden against the Utah Jazz. The next morning, the team was hit with the

(*From left to right*), Danilo Gallinari, Raymond Felton, Amar'e Stoudemire, and Shawne Williams of the New York Knicks in January 2011

devastating news that Stoudemire's brother had been killed in a car crash in Florida. Stoudemire immediately left the Knicks to be with his family there. He would miss the team's next three games. At the Garden that evening, Lin was introduced as a starter at guard to the roar of the sold-out crowd, which included half a dozen newly crowned Super Bowl champion New York Giants. Six minutes into the game, Anthony suffered a groin injury and was lost for the game. Before long, center Chandler was on the bench with foul trouble. No star players left for the Knicks? No problem. They had Jeremy Lin.

Leading a cast of mostly second-teamers, Jeremy smartly directed the offense by spreading the floor, driving hard to the basket, and kicking out to open shooters. He recorded career highs with twenty-eight points and eight assists while raising the play of backups like Steve Novak, who scored a season-best nineteen.

The crowd chanted his name throughout the night, and it was loudest in the fourth quarter when Jeremy single-handedly seized control of a game the Knicks barely led, 75-73, to start the period. He started by taking a pass from Shumpert and scooting down the lane for a layup, foul, and three-point play. He kept the Knicks ahead with another layup and more deft passing and then, with 4:28 left, he made the play of the night. He sliced to his left past Raja Bell to the basket, only to be confronted by Al Jefferson. At the last instant, he switched to his right hand for a reverse. The ball went through the basket as he was fouled, and he converted the free throw for a ten-point lead. Chants of "M-V-P!" echoed through the building. The Jazz cut the lead to six, but Lin iced it moments later. He caught a tap-out from Chandler and launched a three-pointer to beat the twenty-four-second shot clock. The ball ripped through the net for a 95-86 lead with 1:58 left. Coach D'Antoni raised his fists in triumph.

Lin drives the ball to the basket next to Utah Jazz's Al Jefferson during the second half of an NBA basketball game in New York.

Jeremy smiled as he backpedaled, then playfully stuck out his tongue and winked. The Knicks won, 99-88.

Lin did commit eight turnovers, all in the second half, but it was likely due to exhaustion. He played forty-five of the game's forty-eight minutes. "I'm riding him like freaking Secretariat," D'Antoni said, referring to the most powerful racehorse ever. After Lin hit the clinching three-pointer with less than two minutes left, D'Antoni wanted to rest him. "I was going to take him out," said the coach, "and he looked at me and said, 'I don't want to come out.'" Lin had created an instant love affair with New York. Everyone started using a new phrase: *Linsanity!* It was a word invented that day by the Knicks marketing department in an e-mail sent to fans. "God works in mysterious and miraculous ways," Lin said with a smile in the locker room. The outcome seemed all the more stunning with the Knicks missing their stars. "Basketball's so fun when you play on a team where people want to work together and work through tough times and overcome them and have victories like this," Lin said. "This team has a lot of will."

Lin really was speaking about himself.

Fans hold a sign about Lin during the first half of the Los Angeles Lakers-Phoenix Suns NBA basketball game in Phoenix.

five
Linsanity

L insanity had erupted. Lin's story was on the front page of newspapers and the lead story on television sports highlights shows. How could an unknown bench warmer burst onto the scene this way? "I don't think anyone, including myself, saw this coming," Lin said after his game against the Jazz, in which he became the first player in more than thirty years to record at least twenty-eight points and eight assists in his first NBA start. He was suddenly the top trending topic on Twitter in New York and San Francisco. The day of the Jazz game, he picked up nearly 10,000 followers on his account, @JLin7. The day after, a Lin-themed hip-hop song appeared on YouTube. His popularity transcended Knicks fans. He represented a point of pride among Asian Americans. He connected with devout Christians because he spoke openly of his faith, much like quarterback Tim Tebow, another recent evangelical sports phenomenon. He resonated with Harvard and Ivy Leaguers. He represented the underdog. The

Tim Tebow "tebowing," a phrase referring to his kneeling in prayer

Knicks guaranteed his contract, of course, and he set out in search of his own apartment. He found one in lower Manhattan near the World Trade Center site.

What made Lin achieve this sudden success? Two reasons. He could get to the basket and he could run the pick-and-roll. He had long known such moves as the crossover dribble, the hesitation dribble, and the basic spin. What he lacked was the explosiveness to perform these moves in a flash. That is, until he began that intense strength program after his rookie season. By increasing his strength and the spring in his step, he could blow by defenders now. Also, it was no secret that Coach D'Antoni was a master of pick-and-roll plays. Lin's hard work in the D-League while with the Warriors, where he learned to use the entire floor, was paying dividends now. Former Knicks coach and NBA analyst Jeff Van Gundy said, "He's galvanized their team. He's made his teammates run harder on the break and cut harder in half court offense because they now know they'll be rewarded when they do so. In the pick-and-roll, he makes very good decisions. He knows when to pass, he knows when to shoot, and he does both very well."

Two days after the Jazz game, Lin and the Knicks traveled to Washington, D.C., to play the Wizards. So many fans at the Verizon Center wore Lin jerseys and held signs that it felt almost like a Knicks home game. "Are You Not—Lin-Tertained?" read one poster. "Super Lintendo Entertainment System" read another. Five Asian Americans wore blue shirts with orange lettering, spelling out "LIN 17." The Knicks were missing Stoudemire, who was still in Florida, as well as their leading scorer Anthony, who would miss two weeks with his injury. Lin would have to direct mostly second-teamers again.

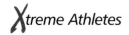

In the first quarter, Wizard guard John Wall crashed into Lin, opening a gash on his chin. Lin was taken to the bench, where he spent the next few minutes getting bandaged by the team trainer. The Knicks fell behind by eight points. Early in the second quarter, he returned to the court and restored order. He penetrated to the rim, dished out to Novak for three-pointers, and fed Chandler inside. The Knicks were up by six at the half. Late in the third quarter, Lin juked past his defender, slithered into the lane, and rose for a driving one-handed dunk. The Knicks bench and screaming fans jumped to their feet. Lin smiled and admitted later that he hadn't dunked since the D-League in Reno. He continued to dominate as the Knicks pulled away. Chants of "Jeremy Lin!" filled the arena, and with 1:44 left and the Knicks ahead by sixteen, he was subbed off the court to one last roar. The Knicks won, 107-93. Lin finished with twenty-three points and a new career-high ten assists. He committed just two turnovers. In New York's locker room, all the praise was for Jeremy. "You can see it in all our faces," Jared Jeffries said. "The energy in this room, the camaraderie right now that we have, that he's kind of unified this team. He's what we needed, the whole time."

Kobe Bryant

The excitement reached a crescendo two nights later back in New York City. Kobe Bryant and the Los Angeles Lakers were in town. America's largest city craves star power, and fans delighted in watching Bryant, once considered the league's brightest star, perform his magic. Bryant had been asked the night before what he thought about Linsanity. "I have no idea what you guys are talking about," he replied. The back page of the *New York Daily News* captured the hype with the headline: "The Mighty Lin: Forget About Kobe. Knick Sensation Headlines Garden Tonight." The *New York Post* headline screamed: "May the Best Man Lin. Jeremy vs. Kobe Tonight at MSG." The game was televised nationally, and millions of people who don't ordinarily watch basketball tuned in to see what the fuss was all about. Millions more watched

As Linsanity took off, souvenir shops around New York began selling his jersey to the masses.

on Asian TV. Souvenir shops inside the arena sold out of "Lin" jerseys before the game started. The Knicks were missing Stoudemire and Anthony again, but that didn't matter now. Lin scored his team's first basket by hitting a three-pointer, and the crowd went crazy. He passed to Chandler for a layup and a dunk and scored nine of his team's first thirteen points. The fans chanted "Jer-e-my!"

Lin scored as many first-quarter baskets as the entire Lakers team, and the Knicks stretched their lead to fourteen early in the second quarter. When the Lakers got to within five, Lin stopped the rally, finding Chandler for a layup, then hitting a turn-around jumper and spinning on Derek Fisher for a layup. He kept the Knicks in front through the third quarter before finally getting a much-needed rest to start the fourth. With 9:25 to go, the Lakers crept to within three points. He returned and blew past Bryant for a dunk to bring more roars from the crowd. Later, he drilled a long jumper, then buried a three-pointer from the wing to make it 84-71. The Lakers called timeout, and for the full two-minute break, fans stood shouting, as though it were the seventh game of the NBA Finals. The Lakers clawed back once more to make it 88-82 and with fifty-two seconds left, Lin stepped to the free throw line and calmly sank both shots amid booming chants of "M-V-P! M-V-P!" The Knicks won, 92-85. Lin scored thirty-eight points to set a Knicks season record for most points in game. Lin tried to down-play his amazing performance. "The only thing we established tonight is four in a row," he said. "Now we try to go for five tomorrow. I'm not too worried about proving anything to anybody." Everyone else involved spoke more frankly. "What he's doing is

amazing," said coach D'Antoni. "He answered a lot of questions tonight. Can he make an outside shot? Can he pull the trigger in a big moment? There's so much stuff that he's doing." The Knicks coach tried to grasp the enormity of it all. "This is a once-in-a-lifetime thing," he said. "I don't know what to tell you. I've never seen it." Bryant was effusive with his praise, saying, "I think it's a great story. It's a testament to perseverance and hard work. I think it's a good example for kids everywhere."

Lin's story gripped athletes from all sports. "Who is this guy? Where'd they find him," New York Giants lineman Justin Tuck asked friends as he rode down an arena elevator. "If he's still looking for a place to crash," said New York Yankees slugger Alex Rodriguez, "he can crash at my apartment. Imagine the tabloids then." Tennis star Roger Federer simply said, "This is why we all follow sports." The celebration over Lin was rampant and far-reaching. From Times Square to Taipei, his story was all the rage. Even his eighty-five-year-old grandmother in Taiwan was being stalked by paparazzi.

Because of his injury, Carmelo Anthony was not an active part of his team's newfound success, and some wondered how he felt about it. He was born in Brooklyn's projects and played at Syracuse

Lin's Taiwanese grandmother, Lin Ju An-mian, in a sports bar in downtown Taipei, Taiwan, watching her grandson play basketball and sharing old photographs of him as a child

in upstate New York. After toiling for eight years with the Denver Nuggets, he joined his hometown Knicks a year earlier, and the spotlight had been cast his way ever since. "It's crazy," said Anthony. "Everywhere you go, it's Lin, Lin, Lin, Lin. I'm actually enjoying it." Whether Anthony minded or not, he didn't dare say, for the sake of appearing petty. The truth was, his game was not conducive to the up-tempo team-basketball style that Lin was operating. Anthony was highly skilled at the isolation play, in which his teammates would clear out and watch him go one-on-one. The sharpest Knicks

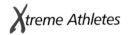

fans knew that his return to the court might conflict with the offense. And what about the teams that waived Lin just two months earlier? Warriors general manager Larry Riley confessed, "I have egg on my face in telling you that I did not think he was going to become a starting point guard with a good team. He's doing that now." Rockets general manager Daryl Morey wrote on Twitter, "We should have kept @JLin7. Did not know he was this good. Anyone who says they knew misleading U."

The Knicks were in Minnesota the following night, and before the game, Timberwolves guard Ricky Rubio said about Lin, "He's been amazing. He's smart and a great kid. We'll try to stop him." Lin dazzled the crowd early with a crossover move and step-back jumper, a teardrop in the lane, and a stutter-step blow-by for two more. But from then, Rubio and others launched a suffocating defense on him, and Lin struggled to get decent shots. He did score twenty points to lead his team, but on just 8-of-24 shooting. The Knicks trailed by eight at the half and were still down seven with 6:41 left. They clawed back and finally tied it at ninety-eight when Lin kicked out a pass to Novak for three with thirty-six seconds left. After a steal, the clock ticked down with the ball in Lin's hands once more.

He drove hard and drew a foul on Luke Ridnour with four seconds left. He missed the first free throw but made the next one to win the game. After another Timberwolves turnover with one second left, Bill Walker added a free throw for a 100-98 final. "It was a gutsy one," Lin said. "Everybody was tired. We never gave up."

The nail-biting victory was New York's fifth in a row. But it didn't compare to the drama that came next. In Canada for their next game against the Toronto Raptors, the media clamoring to report on the saga overwhelmed the Knicks. At a morning press conference, seventy-five reporters and sixteen cameras crammed the pressroom, including twenty-five Chinese Canadian journalists. "Are we in the playoffs now?" coach D'Antoni quipped as he stepped to the microphone. A season-high crowd of more than 20,000 filled the arena that night to see Linsanity. Instead, they watched their hometown Raptors take a commanding seventeen-point lead. The Knicks cut into the deficit but still trailed by nine with under four minutes to go. Lin's free throw started a comeback. He would finish with a game-high twenty-seven points and a career-high eleven assists, but it was his heroics at the end that will be forever remembered.

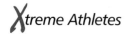

Down 87-84 with one minute left, he took a pass from Shumpert and popped in a difficult four-footer as he was getting fouled. He converted the free throw to tie it. After a Raptors miss, Shumpert missed for the Knicks, but Chandler secured the offensive rebound with twenty seconds left. The ball was given to Lin. The crowd stood as he dribbled at the top of the key, just beyond the three-point arc. Leandro Barbosa guarded him. Lin watched the clocked tick down . . . 5 seconds . . . 4 . . . 3 . . . 2. He rose up and launched the three-pointer at the height of his jump, just as he'd learned playing "beat the ghost." Bang! The ball ripped through the net for the winning shot. The crowd broke into a frenzy as the Knicks swarmed their hero. "You just watch and you're in awe," D'Antoni said. Lin deflected praise. He maintained a humble character. "It's not because of me. It's because we're coming together as a team," he said. "I'm thankful that the coach and my teammates trust me with the ball at the end of the game. I'm just very thankful."

Back at Madison Square Garden for a game the next night, Linsanity was at a fever pitch. At the city's hot spots, Asian Americans who had never followed Knicks games were cheering every basket. Lin's jersey was far and away the top-seller in the league now. The NBA had shipped his jerseys to twenty-three countries. Bids for his rookie card exceeded $21,000 on eBay. On the social network Sina, China's version of Twitter, Lin

A collection of New York City newspaper front pages showing the popularity of Jeremy Lin

surpassed 1 million followers. He appeared on the cover of *Sports Illustrated* for the second week in a row. He was informed that even President Barack Obama was talking about him. "I mean, wow, the President. Nothing better than that," he replied. "I'm very honored, very humbled." With Lin recording a season-high thirteen assists, the Knicks bolted out to an eighteen-point halftime lead against the Sacramento Kings, allowing their new star to sit for some needed rest much of the second half. New York's 100-85 win was its seventh straight and evened its record at 15-15.

Record-Breaker

By scoring twenty-eight points against the Utah Jazz, twenty-three against the Washington Wizards, and thirty-eight against the Los Angeles Lakers, for a total of eighty-nine, Jeremy Lin broke the New York Knicks post-merger record for most points in his first three starts. Bill Cartwright had scored eighty in his first three games in 1980, and Patrick Ewing had sixty-four in 1985.

After his dominating game against the Lakers, Lin tied LeBron James for most consecutive games (four) with at least two points, five assists, and a shooting percentage of 50.0 or higher.

After hitting the winning shot at Toronto, Lin reached twenty points and seven assists for the sixth straight game—the longest streak in the NBA of the season. It was also the longest streak in New York Knicks history.

Lin scored 136 points in his first five starts, the most by any NBA player since the NBA merged with the ABA in 1976. His total broke the mark of 129 points set by Shaquille O'Neal twenty years earlier.

Then the streak ended. Lin scored a game-high twenty-six points, but he committed nine turnovers to hurt his team in an 89-85 loss to the lowly New Orleans Hornets. Lin was quick to accept blame. "Just a lackluster effort on my part and careless with the ball," he said. It didn't help that the team missed twenty of its twenty-four three-point shots. Afterward, ESPN used a racial slur on its mobile Web site with the headline "Chink in the Armor." The headline was removed within thirty-five minutes, and the employee who posted the headline was fired.

Two nights later, Linsanity was back on course. Fans along the front rows included actors Kevin Costner and Eva Longoria, Facebook co-founder Mark Zuckerberg, Lin's high school coach, Peter Diepenbrock, and, of course, avid Knicks fan Spike Lee, who wore Lin's number four Harvard jersey. They watched Lin torch the defending champion Dallas Mavericks for twenty-eight points and a career-high fourteen assists, as the Knicks stormed back from twelve points down in the third quarter to win, 104-97.

The following night's game against the Nets marked the return of Carmelo Anthony. Baron Davis also played his first game for the Knicks after recovering from a back injury. Davis was penciled in to

Lin drives past Boston Celtics' Kevin Garnett as Celtics' Rajon Rondo watches during overtime in an NBA basketball game in Boston, on March 4, 2012.

become the team's point guard before the arrival of Linsanity. In the game, Lin scored twenty-one points and had nine assists and seven rebounds, but Anthony went 4-for-11 for eleven points and Davis had just three points in nine minutes in a backup role. The Knicks lost, 100-92. They recovered with a win over the Atlanta Hawks, lost to the eventual champion Miami Heat, and defeated the Cleveland Cavaliers. Then the team went into a tailspin. The Knicks lost in overtime to the Boston Celtics. They lost by ten to the Mavericks, a game in which Anthony shot just 2-of-12. Anthony disagreed with D'Antoni about his role in the offense. The Knicks dropped four more in a row. D'Antoni felt the disruption within his team. He decided to quit. Assistant coach Mike Woodson took over. Woodson preferred an offense that featured isolation plays for Anthony. Some guessed that Davis would become the starting point guard. Woodson said that would not happen–yet. "Right now Jeremy Lin is our starting point guard and Baron is backing him up," said Woodson.

Lin did remain the starter, and he led the Knicks on a five-game winning streak. They split their next two games—losing to the Raptors and beating the Detroit Pistons—and were clinging to the

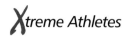

eighth and final playoff spot with seventeen games left in the season. Unfortunately, Lin would not play another game for them. He suffered a knee injury in the second half against Detroit. It was his fourth game in five nights, and he thought the injury was from overuse. Doctors discovered torn cartilage. Lin underwent surgery to repair it. He spent the rest of season watching from the bench in street clothes. He saw the Knicks reach the playoffs but lose in the first round in five games to the Heat.

With the season officially over, Lin's one-year contract was up. He was a restricted free agent. He could sign a deal with any team. The Knicks were allowed to match the deal. They stated that they would match any deal. The Houston Rockets called Lin's agent, Roger Montgomery. Lin was offered a three-year deal worth $25.1 million. Lin signed the deal and waited for the Knicks to respond. The next day, the Knicks made a trade to acquire point guard Raymond Felton from the Portland Trail Blazers. Felton had played for the Knicks two years earlier. Lin was shocked. The Knicks had three days to match Lin's offer or let him go to the Rockets. It was the leading story in the sports world, as experts debated what the Knicks should do. Most said Lin was worth keeping.

On July 18, the Knicks announced their decision to pass on Lin. "Extremely excited and honored to be a Houston Rocket again!!" Lin posted on his Twitter account. "Much love and thankfulness to the Knicks and New York for your support the past year . . . easily the best year of my life."

Lin is confident in any uniform. He has worked tirelessly to be an NBA player. He will continue to improve because he knows no other way. He does not seek glory. Being a global phenomenon is not his purpose. His goal is to help his team win games. "You can fall as fast as you rise. That's just the reality of the situation," Lin says. "I just want to make sure I'm not doing a disservice to my team by milking all the attention and being on the cover of everything. Because at the end of the day, that's not what I love. I love playing basketball. That's my passion."

Lin poses with a Houston Rockets jersey after a news conference on July 19, 2012, in Houston.

TIMELINE

1988	Born August 23 in Los Angeles, California.
1993	Starts playing basketball competitively.
2003	Brought up to varsity for playoffs as a freshman.
2006	Leads Palo Alto High School to state title; enrolls at Harvard.
2009	Leads Harvard to first win over nationally ranked team; sets multiple team records.
2010	Sets multiple Ivy League records; finalist for college basketball Most Valuable Player; becomes fourth Asian American to play in NBA and first of Taiwanese or Chinese decent.
2011	Waived by Golden State Warriors and Houston Rockets; signed by New York Knicks.
2012	Sets multiple NBA individual records.

SOURCES

Chapter One: Learning the Game

p. 10, "to watch the . . ." Dana O'Neil, "Immigrant Dream Plays Out Through Son," ESPN.com, December 10, 2009, http://sports.espn.go.com/ncb/columns/ story?columnist=oneil_dana&id=4730385.

p. 12, "I realized that . . ." Ibid.

p. 13, "He stood at . . ." Sean Gregory, "Harvard's Hoops Star is Asian. Why's That a Problem?," *Time,* December 31, 2009.

p. 13, "I'm going to . . ." Ibid.

p. 13, "From that game . . ." Ibid.

p. 13, "Ever since I . . ." Timothy Dalrymple, "The Faith and Fate of Jeremy Lin," *Evangelical Portal*, March 3, 2010.

p. 14, "We'd run to . . ." "Lin's Journey to Stardom," ESPN, aired February 21, 2012.

p. 15, "My first memory . . ." Ibid.

p. 15, "Honestly, I didn't . . ." Dalrymple, "The Faith and Fate of Jeremy Lin."

p. 15, "Jeremy has a . . ." O'Neil, "Immigrant Dream Plays Out Through Son."

p. 16, "I'm going to . . ." "Old Friend From Skokie Remembers Jeremy Lin From Way Back," Chicago.cbslocal.com, March 12, 2012, http://chicago.cbslocal. com/2012/03/12/old-friend-from-skokie-remembers-jeremy-lin-from-way-back/.

p. 16, "Go back to . . ." O'Neil, "Immigrant Dream Plays Out Through Son."

p. 16, "Open your eyes . . ." Bryan Chu, "Asian Americans Remain Rare in Men's College Basketball," *San Francisco Chronicle*, December 16, 2008.

p. 16, "It was definitely . . ." Ibid.

p. 17, "I told him . . ." Ibid.

p. 17, "I was just . . ." "Lin's Journey to Stardom," ESPN.

p. 17, "It caused me . . ." Ibid.

p. 19, "he was so happy . . ." Ibid.

pp. 20-21, "We would talk . . ." Dalrymple, "The Faith and Fate of Jeremy Lin."

p. 22, "We knew all ..." Jay Caspian King, "Person of Interest: Jeremy Lin – A Trip Deep Into the Heart of Linsanity," *Grantland*, February 13, 2012.

pp. 22-23, "But hey, I . . ." Ibid.

p. 23, "We can't give . . ." Mark Viera, "For Lin, Erasing a History of Being Overlooked," *New York Times*, February 12, 2012.

p. 23, "He was a . . ." Ibid.

p. 23, "I just think . . ."Ibid.

p. 24, "It's the Asian . . ." King, "Person of Interest: Jeremy Lin–A Trip Deep Into the Heart of Linsanity."

p. 25, "He didn't really . . ." Chris Dortch, "Harvard was Perfect Place for Lin to Hone Guard Skills," NBA.com., February 17, 2012, http://www.nba.com/2012/news/fea-tures/chris_dortch/02/17/lin-college-break/index.html.

p. 25, "He was able . . ." Ibid.

p. 25, "I just really . . ." "Lin's Journey to Stardom," ESPN.

Chapter Two: Harvard Education

p. 28, "the weakest guy . . ." Howard Beck, "The Evolution of a Point Guard," *New York Times*, February 24, 2012.

p. 30, "Wonton soup," Pablo S. Torre, "Harvard School of Basketball," *Sports Illustrated*, February 1, 2010.

p. 30,   "Sweet and sour . . ." Gregory, "Harvard's Hoops Star is Asian. Why's That a Problem?"

p. 30,   "Go back to . . ." Chu, "Asian Americans Remain Rare in Men's College Basketball."

p. 30,   "It's everything you . . ." Gregory, "Harvard's Hoops Star is Asian. Why's That a Problem?"

p. 30,   "They're yelling at . . ." Chu, "Asian Americans Remain Rare in Men's College Basketball."

p. 30,   "Sorry, sir . . ." Gwen Knapp, "Bay Area Appeal Makes Lin Good Bet," *San Francisco Chronicle*, July 22, 2010.

p. 31,   "We are called . . ." Dalrymple, "The Faith and Fate of Jeremy Lin."

p. 31,   "I learned more . . ." Ibid.

p. 32,   "The way he . . ." Bill Gutman, *Jeremy Lin – The Incredible Rise of the NBA's Most Unlikely Superstar* (New York: Sports Publishing, 2012), 25.

p. 32,   "He was just . . ." Ibid., 26.

p. 33,   "Jeremy was a . . ." Dortch, "Harvard was Perfect Place for Lin to Hone Guard Skills."

p. 34,   "Lin Powers Harvard to Rare Upset Over No. 24 BC," Associated Press, January 7, 2009, ESPN Men's Basketball, http://scores.espn.go.com/ncb/recap?gameId=290070103.

p. 36,   "He's a special . . ." Gregory, "Harvard's Hoops Star is Asian. Why's That a Problem?"

p. 37,   "He's as consistent . . ." O'Neil, "Immigrant Dream Plays Out Through Son."

p. 38,   "I've seen a lot . . ." Ibid.

p. 38,   "There are times . . ." Dalrymple, "The Faith and Fate of Jeremy Lin."

p. 40,   "It's a sport . . ." Chu, "Asian Americans Remain Rare in Men's College Basketball."

p. 40,   "Right away, I . . ." Neil Janowitz, "After Backing a Dark Horse, Lin's Agent is Riding High," *New York Times*, March 9, 2012.

p. 40,   "There are very few . . ." Adam Himmelsbach, "Basketball Grad School for 3 Ivy League Stars," *New York Times*, April 10, 2010.

p. 42,   "some Steve Nash- . . ." Ibid.

p. 43,   "I guess he . . ." Rusty Simmons, "Jeremy Lin – the Story Just Keeps Getting Better," *San Francisco Chronicle*, Thursday, July 22, 2010.

p. 43,   "I was devastated . . ." Ibid.

p. 43,   "I was very . . ." "Lin's Journey to Stardom," ESPN.

Chapter Three: Not Giving Up

p. 46,   "Donnie took care . . ." Simmons, "Jeremy Lin–the Story Just Keeps Getting Better."

pp. 46-47, "That was by . . ." Martin Kessler, "Jeremy Lin To Sign With Warriors, Reports Say," *Harvard Crimson*, July 20, 2010.

p. 47,   "He showed us . . ." Marc Stein, "Sources: Lin Near Deal With Warriors," ESPN.com, July 21, 2010, http://sports.espn.go.com/nba/news/story?id=5396732.

p. 48,   "It was surprising . . ." Anna Katherine Clemmons, "Jeremy Lin: NBA's Cinderella Story," ESPN.com, February 11, 2012, http://m.espn.go.com/nba/story?storyId=6099342&wjb=.

p. 50,   "I've got news . . ." Marcus Thompson II, "Paly Grad Lin Captivates Warriors Crowd in Brief Appearance," *San Jose Mercury News*, October 9, 2010.

p. 50,   "He's getting to . . ." Beck, "The Evolution of a Point Guard."

p. 50,   "All of a sudden . . ." Ibid.

p. 51,   "We want Lin!" Clemmons, "Jeremy Lin: NBA's Cinderella Story."

p. 51,   "I sat on . . ." Bob Fitzgerald, "Jeremy Lin Q&A After Warriors vs. Clippers Game," Interview, YouTube.com, October 29, 2010, http://www.youtube.com/watch?v=qnpsJ7zGjDk.

pp. 51-52, "I'm thankful to . . ." Ryan Leong, "Jeremy Lin Steals the Show at Warriors Asian Heritage Night," *San Francisco Examiner*, October 30, 2010.

p. 52,   "I'm not going . . ." J. Michael Falgoust, "Golden State's Jeremy Lin Scores One for the Ivys," *USA TODAY*, November 1, 2010.

pp. 52-53, "I am a . . ." Rick Quan, "Rex Walters," Quanmansports'schannel, YouTube.com, May 11, 2011, http://www.youtube.com/watch?v=o4b0nLia7c0.

p. 54,   "He plays with . . ." Ibid.

p. 55,   "I've never seen . . ." Clemmons, "Jeremy Lin: NBA's Cinderella Story."

p. 55,   "There's a lot . . ." Rusty Simmons, "Stop Cheering For Jeremy Lin," *San Francisco Chronicle*, November 2, 2010.

p. 56,   "When I'm on . . ." Ibid.

p. 56,   "Jeremy couldn't shoot . . ." Beck, "The Evolution of a Point Guard."

p. 57,   "I thought he . . ." Ibid.

p. 57,   "That was the . . ." Ibid.

p. 59,   "That's the beauty . . ." Ibid.

p. 59,   "Before, he was . . ." Ibid.

Chapter Four: Seizing the Opportunity

p. 64,   "It was a calculated . . ." Marcus Thompson II, "Golden State Warriors Notebook: Stephen Curry Misses Practice With Bad Ankle," *San Jose Mercury News*, December 27, 2011.

p. 65,   "If I don't . . ." "Lin's Journey to Stardom," ESPN.

p. 65,   "When I saw . . ." Neil Janowitz, "After Backing a Dark Horse, Lin's Agent is Riding High," *New York Times*, March 9, 2012.

p. 65,   "We did like . . ." Howard Beck, "Lin's Success Surprising to Everyone," *New York Times*, February 9, 2012.

pp. 65-66, "We didn't know . . ." Ibid.

p. 66,   "Everything I expected . . ." Thompson II, "Golden State Warriors Notebook: Stephen Curry Misses Practice With Bad Ankle."

p. 66,   "He's from Harvard . . ." Howard Beck, "Knicks' Strengths Vanish, and So Do Hopes of Winning," *New York Times,* December 29, 2011.

p. 67,   "If somebody wakes . . ." Howard Beck, "Hit by Injuries, Knicks Add Former Harvard Guard," *New York Times*, December 27, 2011.

p. 68,   "I'm still kind . . ." Howard Beck, "Newest Knick Out to Prove He's Not Just a Novelty," *New York Times*, December 28, 2012.

p. 75,   "A little overwhelmed . . ." Howard Beck, "Lin Sparks Knicks, To Crowd's Delight and D'Antoni's Relief," *New York Times*, February 4, 2012.

p. 75,   "What's going on? . . ." Ibid.

p. 75,   "phenomenal," "Jeremy Lin Shines as Knicks Bounce Back Against Nets," Associated Press, February 5, 2012.

p. 75,   "The biggest thing . . ." Beck, "Lin Sparks Knicks, To Crowd's Delight and D'Antoni's Relief."

p. 79,   "I'm riding him . . ." Howard Beck, "Knicks' Lin Fires Up Garden With 28 Points in First Start," *New York Times*, February 6, 2012.

p. 79,   "God works in . . ." Ibid.

p. 79,   "Basketball's so fun . . ." "Knicks Overcome Carmelo Anthony Injury as Jeremy
             Lin Hangs Career-High 28 on Jazz," ESPN.com, February 6, 2012, http://espn.
             go.com/nba/recap?gameId=320206018.

Chapter Five: Linsanity

p. 81,   "I don't think . . ." Howard Beck, "From Ivy Halls to the Garden, Surprise Star Jolts
             the NBA," *New York Times*, February 7, 2012.
p. 83,   "He's galvanized their . . ." "Lin's Journey to Stardom," ESPN.
p. 84,   "You can see . . ." Howard Beck, "Lin Leads Again as Knicks Win Third in a Row,"
             New York Times, February 8, 2012.
p. 85,   "I have no idea . . ." "Lin's Journey to Stardom," ESPN.
p. 85,   "The Mighty Lin . . ." *New York Daily News*, February 10, 2012.
p. 85,   "May the Best . . ." *New York Post*, February 10, 2012.
p. 87,   "The only thing . . ." "Jeremy Lin Pours in Career-Best 38 Points, Leads
             Knicks Past Lakers," ESPN.com, February 10, 2012, http://espn.go.com/nba/
             recap?gameId=320210018.
pp. 87-88,   "What he's doing . . ." Ibid.
p. 88,   "This is a . . ." Howard Beck, "With 38 Points, the Legend Grows," *New York Times*,
             February 10, 2012.
p. 88,   "I think it's . . ." Ibid.
p. 88,   "Who is this . . ." Harvey Araton, "Lin Keeps His Cool; Around Him, Heads Spin,"
             New York Times, February 12, 2012.
p. 88,   "If he's still . . ." "David Stern Fascinated by Jeremy Lin," Associated Press,
             February 24, 2012.
p. 88,   "This is why . . ." Ibid.
p. 89,   "It's crazy . . ." "Lin's Journey to Stardom," ESPN.
p. 90,   "I have egg . . ." Howard Beck, "Lin's Success Surprising to Everyone," *New York
             Times*, February 9, 2012.
p. 90,   "We should have . . ." Ibid.
p. 90,   "He's been amazing . . ." Brian Mahoney, "Linsanity: Knicks Benchwarmer
             Becomes a Star," Associated Press, February 12, 2012.
p. 91,   "It was a gutsy . . ." "Jeremy Lin Leads Knicks By Wolves for Fifth Straight Win,"
             Associated Press, February 11, 2012.
p. 91,   "Are we in . . ." "Jeremy Lin Hits Game-Winning 3 as Knicks Top Raptors,"
             Associated Press, February 14, 2012.
p. 92,   "You just watch . . ." Ibid.
p. 92,   "It's not because . . ." Ibid.
p. 93,   "I mean, wow . . ." Andy Katz and Ian Begley, "President
             Obama Watching Jeremy Lin," ESPNNewYork.com, February
             16, 2012, http://espn.go.com/new-york/nba/story/_/id/7578530/
             president-barack-obama-david-stern-tracking-new-york-knicks-pg-jeremy-lin.
p. 95,   "Just a lackluster . . ." "Hornets Slow Down Jeremy Lin, Snap Knicks' Winning
             Streak," Associated Press, February 17, 2012.
p. 97,   "Right now Jeremy . . ." Ian Begley, "Jeremy Lin Still Knicks Starter,"
             ESPNNewYork.com, March 16, 2012, http://m.espn.go.com/nba/
             story?storyId=7696738&e=RAD.
p. 99.   "Extremely excited and honored . . ." Ian Begley, "Knicks Let Rockets Land Jeremy
             Lin," ESPNNewYork.com, July 17, 2012, http://espn.go.com/new-york/nba/story/_/
             id/8175591/new-york-knicks-confirm-match-houston-rockets-offer-jeremy-lin.
p. 99,   "You can fall . . ." *Lin's Journey to Stardom*, ESPN.

BIBLIOGRAPHY

Araton, Harvey. "Lin Keeps His Cool; Around Him, Heads Spin." *New York Times*, February 12, 2012.

Associated Press. "Jeremy Lin Shines as Knicks Bounce Back Against Nets." February 5, 2012.

———. "Jeremy Lin Leads Knicks By Wolves for Fifth Straight Win." February 11, 2012.

———. "Jeremy Lin Hits Game-Winning 3 as Knicks Top Raptors." February 14, 2012.

———. "Hornets Slow Down Jeremy Lin, Snap Knicks' Winning Streak." February 17, 2012.

———. "David Stern Fascinated by Jeremy Lin." February 24, 2012.

Beck, Howard. "Hit by Injuries, Knicks Add Former Harvard Guard," *New York Times*, December 27, 2011.

———. "Newest Knick Out to Prove He's Not Just a Novelty." *New York Times*, December 28, 2012.

———. "Knicks' Strengths Vanish, and So Do Hopes of Winning. December 29, 2011.

———. "Lin Sparks Knicks, To Crowd's Delight and D'Antoni's Relief." *New York Times*, February 4, 2012.

———. "Knicks' Lin Fires Up Garden With 28 Points in First Start." *New York Times*, February 6, 2012.

———. "From Ivy Halls to the Garden, Surprise Star Jolts the NBA." *New York Times*, February 7, 2012.

———. "Lin Leads Again as Knicks Win Third in a Row." *New York Times*, February 8, 2012.

———. "Lin's Success Surprising to Everyone." *New York Times*, February 9, 2012.

———. "With 38 Points, the Legend Grows," *New York Times*, February 10, 2012.

———. "The Evolution of a Point Guard." *New York Times*, February 24, 2012.

Chu, Bryan. "Asian Americans Remain Rare in Men's College Basketball." *San Francisco Chronicle*, December 16, 2008.

Clemmons, Anna Katherine. "Jeremy Lin: NBA's Cinderella Story," ESPN.com, March 16, 2011. http://www.webcitation.org/65fxAT2kq.

Dalrymple, Timothy. "The Faith and Fate of Jeremy Lin." *Evangelical Portal*, March 3, 2010.

Dortch, Chris. "Harvard was Perfect Place for Lin to Hone Guard Skills." NBA.com. http://www.nba.com/2012/news/features/chris_dortch/02/17/lin-college-break/index.html.

ESPN.com. "Knicks Overcome Carmelo Anthony Injury as Jeremy Lin Hangs Career-High 28 on Jazz." ESPN.com, February 6, 2012. http://espn.go.com/nba/recap?gameId=320206018.

———. "Jeremy Lin Pours in Career-Best 38 Points, Leads Knicks Past Lakers." February 10, 2012, http://espn.go.com/nba/recap?gameId=320210018.

ESPN. *Lin's Journey to Stardom*, February 21, 2012.

Chicago.cbslocal.com, "Old Friend From Skokie Remembers Jeremy Lin From Way Back." March 12, 2012.

Falgoust, Michael J. "Golden State's Jeremy Lin Scores One for the Ivys." *USA TODAY*, November 1, 2010.

Fitzgerald, Bob. "Jeremy Lin Q&A After Warriors vs. Clippers Game." Interview, October 29, 2010, YouTube., http://www.youtube.com/watch?v=qnpsJ7zGjDk.

Gregory, Sean. "Harvard's Hoops Star is Asian. Why's That a Problem?" *Time*, December 31, 2009.

Gutman, Bill. *Jeremy Lin – The Incredible Rise of the NBA's Most Unlikely Superstar.* New York: Sports Publishing, 2012.

Janowitz, Neil. "After Backing a Dark Horse, Lin's Agent is Riding High." *New York Times*, March 9, 2012.

Katz, Andy, and Ian Begley. "President Obama Watching Jeremy Lin."

Kessler, Martin. "Jeremy Lin To Sign With Warriors, Reports Say." *Harvard Crimson*, July 20, 2010.

King, Jay Caspian. "Person of Interest: Jeremy Lin–A Trip Deep Into the Heart of Linsanity." *Grantland*, February 13, 2012.

Knapp, Gwen. "Bay Area Appeal Makes Lin Good Bet." *San Francisco Chronicle*, July 22, 2010.

Leong, Ryan. "Jeremy Lin Steals the Show at Warriors Asian Heritage Night." *San Francisco Examiner*, October 30, 2010.

Mahoney, Brian. "Linsanity: Knicks Benchwarmer Becomes a Star." Associated Press, February 12, 2012.

O'Neil, Dana. "Immigrant Dream Plays Out Through Son." ESPN.com, December 10, 2009.

Simmons, Rusty. "Jeremy Lin–the Story Just Keeps Getting Better." *San Francisco Chronicle*, Thursday, July 22, 2010.

―――. "Stop Cheering For Jeremy Lin." *San Francisco Chronicle*, November 2, 2010.

Stein, Marc. "Sources: Lin Near Deal With Warriors." ESPN.com., July 21, 2010. http://sports.espn.go.com/nba/news/story?id=5396732.

Thompson II, Marcus. "Paly Grad Lin Captivates Warriors Crowd in Brief Appearance." *San Jose Mercury News*, October 9, 2010.

―――. "Golden State Warriors notebook: Stephen Curry Misses Practice With Bad Ankle." *San Jose Mercury News*, December 27, 2011.

Torre, Pablo S. "Harvard School of Basketball." *Sports Illustrated*, February 1, 2010.

Viera, Mark. "For Lin, Erasing a History of Being Overlooked." *New York Times*, February 12, 2012.

WEB SITES

http://www.jeremylin.com

Jeremy Lin's official site. It includes his biography, photos, recent news about him, and information about Linsanity products, including an online store.

http://www.nba.com

The National Basketball Association official site. It includes recent news, game results, schedules, overviews of players and coaches, and information about teams.

www.nba.com/rockets

This Web site provides information on current and former players and coaches, team and individual statistics, game results, upcoming schedule, and tickets.

INDEX

PHOTO CREDITS